HEAVENLY ANGEL

LAY LAY

AND

GUARDIAN ANGEL

SHADOW

GUESS THE REAL AGE

OF THE EARTH

PUBLISHING COMPANY

ISBN: 978-0-6151-7488-4

www.crossover-ministries-publishing.com

TABLE OF CONTENTS

ANCIENT MYSTERIES SOLVED

MOSES

BIBLIOGRAPHY

ABOUT THE AUTHOR

I was dedicated to Jesus Christ of Nazareth as an infant and accepted Him as my Lord and Savior around seven years old when a visiting youth group led me in prayer at the alter. During my Salvation Prayer I asked Jesus to use me in a special ministry. Something that very few other Christians would want to do. I saw all the people just sitting in the pews, the ushers, and the Sunday School teachers and realized any Christian could do that. I wanted something different. One day in church service there was a visiting minister at a church I was visiting as well. The Minister said, "Jesus is going to make you a 'Healer of a Heart'". Then he asked me if I knew what that meant. I said, "No." the minister said, "I don't either, but whatever it is, Jesus is going to use you in a powerful way.

Helping Rachael, Jesus showed me what a 'Healer of the Heart' is. During the course of me helping Rachael to the 'Promised Land', a real Heavenly Angel named Lay Lay and I were allowed one hour one day to talk about Spiritual and Family situations from the King James Version of the Word of God. These books are designed to answer a lot of Spiritual Questions not even your minister can answer or your Church Denomination. I know theology Doctors who can't tell you how people other than Noah and his family made it past the 'Great Flood', yet their names are listed in the King James Version of the Word of God right after the 'World Wide Flood'. These books explain that and much more. I have written these books to tell the whole truth about the Word of God no matter how difficult it may be for me or others. Yes, there are things I write in these books that I don't even like, but in all fairness and total honestly, I must say the WHOLE TRUTH. The title of this book is 100% real. HEAVENLY ANGEL LAY LAY explained to me these facts.

INTRODUCTION

The first section of this book talks about a few mysteries solved about the Earth and other planets. The second section of this book talks about Moses. All scriptures are taken from the King James Version of the Word of God. This book contains an excerpt from my book. MATTHEW'S WORD 'TWO':REAL WORD OF GOD BIBLE.

BOOKS WRITTEN BY WALTER BURCHETT, BA:

MATTHEW'S WORD 'TWO':REAL WORD OF GOD BIBLE   ISBN: 1-4116-6995-9

HEAVENLY ANGEL LAY LAY EXPLAINS WHY ADAM WAS NEVER CURSED
          ISBN: 978-1-84728-176-0

HEAVENLY ANGEL LAY LAY EXPLAINS WHY ABORTED BABIES DO NOT GO TO HEAVEN
          ISBN: 978-0-6151-7470-9

HEAVENLY ANGEL LAY LAY EXPLAINS THE BIBLICAL GROUNDS FOR MARRIAGE,
          SEPARATION, AND DIVORCE   ISBN: 978-0-6151-7481-5

HEAVENLY ANGEL LAY LAY EXPLAINS WHY PROFESSIONAL COUNSELORS HAVE 'HARDENED
          HEARTS'   ISBN: 978-0-6151-7482-2

HEAVENLY ANGEL LAY LAY EXPLAINS THE DIFFERENCE BETWEEN A 'COLD CHRISTIAN' AND
          A 'BACKSLIDER'   ISBN: 978-0-6151-7483-9

HEAVENLY ANGEL LAY LAY EXPLAINS WHICH BIBLE TO READ, WHICH BIBLE NOT TO READ,
          AND WHY   ISBN: 978-0-6151-7484-6

HEAVENLY ANGEL LAY LAY EXPLAINS WHY GAYS, LESBIANS, BI-SEXUALS, AND
          TRANSSEXUALS DO NOT GO TO HEAVEN   ISBN: 978-0-6151-7485-3

HEAVENLY ANGEL LAY LAY EXPLAINS WHY CHILDREN AND SPORTS ARE DEFINITELY A
          RELIGION IN TODAY'S SOCIETY   ISBN: 978-0-6151-7486-0

HEAVENLY ANGEL LAY LAY EXPLAINS WHAT 'MANY ARE CALLED, BUT FEW ARE CHOSEN
          REALLY MEANS   ISBN: 978-0-6151-7487-7

HEAVENLY ANGEL LAY LAY AND GUARDIAN ANGEL SHADOW GUESS THE REAL AGE OF THE
          EARTH   ISBN: 978-0-6151-7488-4

AN ABUSED MAN'S BATTLES, TRYING TO PROTECT HIS BOYS   ISBN: 978-0-6151-5191-5

HEAVENLY ANGEL

LAY LAY

AND GUARDIAN ANGEL

SHADOW

GUESS THE REAL AGE

OF THE EARTH

PREHISTORIC ANIMALS

I asked, "What about Prehistoric Animals?" Lay Lay said, "There really isn't any such thing as a Prehistoric Animal. All the animals were created on the same day." I asked, "Is there really a "Big Foot." Lay Lay said, "Yes, there really is a 'Big Foot, Sasquach or Abominable Snow Man, whatever term you prefer to call it'. It's a type of a bear, you know like there are Brown Bears, Grizzly Bears, Polar Bears, this particular type of bear just stands on two legs because of the muscles in its back (and legs I think, I know there were two different places the muscles are tighter, but I wasn't familiar with the term of the second place so I cant remember it's name. The back was one place the muscles are tighter I know for sure.) are too tight to walk comfortably on all four legs, so it prefers to walk upright like a human." I asked, "Are there any left?" Lay Lay said, "Yes, there are a few left, they are high up in the snowy mountains, like the Alps for security and protection. They don't like humans so they keep themselves hidden very well and their bodies have adapted to the cold weather. They are vegetarians, meaning they don't eat meat. They eat roots, leaves, etc." I asked, "Are there any in the United States?" Lay Lay said, "I don't think so, remember, I'm just an angel, not God. An angel doesn't know everything, but I haven't ever heard of, or seen any in the United States."

I asked, "What about the dinosaur? There is evidence of them existing." Lay Lay said, "Yes, they existed." Then she said, "Just a minute. I want to ask Shadow about a particular dinosaur." Lay Lay came back and said, "According to Shadow there was one dinosaur still in existence. Everyone knows her as the 'Loc Nes Monster'." She's actually a dinosaur." I asked, "She?" Lay Lay said, "Yes, the Loc Nes Monster is a she. Shadow was over there for a time 'protecting' someone and saw her. That was back in 1969. Shadow doesn't know if she is still alive now, but she was back then. The dinosaurs are found and described in the books of Job Chapter 40:15-24 and Chapter 41, Psalms Chapter 74:13 and 14, Ps 104:26, and Isaiah 27: (KJV). They are called sea monsters, dragons, behemoths (Extremely large hippopotamus.) or leviathans (The characteristics of the dragon.). In the Old Testament people were walking around with the dinosaurs. Look at the characteristics, not the name, just like everything else. Humans get too hung up on titles; they need to look at the characteristics of 'good and evil', not the names or titles."

I asked, "What about the Atheists and Agnostics who want proof of Christ's existence?" Lay Lay said, "They have all kinds of proof, they just don't want to accept it. They already have 'Noah's Ark, the 'Shroud of Christ, and 'the Ark of the Covenant', among other things." I said, "So those really are the real things." Lay Lay said, "Yes, they are the real things. The problem is Atheists and Agnostics don't believe it because of one thing. They want one type of test or another done on everything when the tests themselves are inaccurate. The eruption of Mount Saint Helens gave proof to scientists that the 'Carbon Test' was inaccurate when the Carbon Test was being used. Scientists tested some plants that had 'fossilized' there a few weeks after the eruption . The carbon test said the plants had been fossils for billions of years. The plant fossils couldn't have been billions of years old because the plants were alive and growing just a few weeks before the eruption took place. It was the extreme heat, pressure, and no air, that fossilized the plants. The extreme heat would have burned a plant up, but if the fire can't breathe the plant can't burn. So because there was 'no air' and being covered up by tons of hot molten lava literally flowing over the plants, the plants fossilized instead. Yet the 'Carbon Test' showed the plants had been fossilized for billions of years. Now they are using other tests to try to date Ancient Relics, but there is no way for any test to be accurate because no one really knows how many years ago the Earth was created to begin with. When you use a test that is inaccurate you get inaccurate results. Without an accurate age of the Earth no one can prove how old anything is because there never can be any Empirical Evidence to prove the test is accurate. You should know the definition of 'Empirical Evidence'." I said, "I can para-phrase it for you, 'Empirical Evidence' is when a Scientific Experiment is performed, and in order for it to be Empirical Evidence, the experimenter must be present at the start of the experiment, all the way through the experiment, and at the end of the experiment in order for the 'Results of the Experiment' or 'Evidence of the Experiment' to be truly 'Empirical Evidence'."

I continued, "I remember that, back in the spring of 1980. I was driving back to Stanfield, Oregon from Minot, North Dakota where I attended Northwest Bible College. I drove right through that ash. It went clear into Montana. I heard the news over the radio for about a week that the eruption proved the Carbon Test inaccurate. Then there was no more talk about it. Like it just disappeared." Lay Lay said, "That's because the discovery was covered up. Now what human was around at the beginning, when the Earth was formed when time was still non-existent? The experimenters can't have Empirical Evidence showing how old the Earth is because no human was around then. Not even Adam and Eve. The Earth was made before time ever began." I asked, "Then in your estimation, how old is the Earth, anyway?" Lay Lay said, "Well, we need to take into consideration; as I said before, it was made before time began so whatever number I give you would be just an estimate, not factual." I said, "I understand." Lay Lay said, "It's about 35,000 years old. Remember the scriptures say, 'A day is like a thousand years and a thousand years like a day'. Time was non-existent then, day and night didn't exist then, and calendar years didn't exist then either, remember what happened to Adam and Eve because of the fall, and humans starting to age is when calendar years started." Lay Lay said, "Shadow was listening and asked if you wanted his estimation." I said, "Sure." (Shadow is much more technical than Lay Lay. Shadow and I actually did try to talk to each other, but he really couldn't come down to my level so I could understand what he was saying most of the time. That was before Jesus allowed Lay Lay to come into the picture.) Shadow came out and said, "The Earth is about 40,000 years old." I said, "So the estimated age of Earth is somewhere in around 35,000-40,000 years old." That sure is a lot closer to the actual age of the Earth than any scientist could ever figure out.

I said, "I remember seeing in a movie that Jesus was slapped on the way to being crucified." Lay Lay said, "Yes." I asked, "According to the movie, the man never grew any older and was doomed to live until the Second Coming of Christ. Is that true?" Lay Lay started laughing and said, "No, there was a man who did slap Jesus as you said, but once he did, Jesus looked right into his soul and the man repented right then and there and asked Jesus to be his Lord and Savior. Hollywood has taken the Word of God and created fallacies to down play the actual Life of Christ, and other Biblical Evidence. Don't believe what Hollywood puts out as far as anything like that. Hollywood barely has Jesus turning over the tables when He cleaned out the temple, the movies don't show Jesus getting angry as the scriptures say He really did. Go to the Word of God and ask Him to show you the truth, He will. That's His promise to everyone."

I asked, "Are there other life forms in 'outer space'?" Lay Lay said, "With all those planets out there, why would humans be God's only creation with Free-Will? You already know Heavenly Angels have Free-Will. God didn't take Free-Will from the Fallen Angels when they fell from Heaven, so yes, God has other creation out there with Free-Will."

MOSES CONTINUED

(CONTINUED FROM: HEAVENLY ANGEL LAY LAY EXPLAINS WHAT 'MANY ARE CALLED, BUT FEW ARE CHOSEN' REALLY MEANS)

MOSES

Exodus 21:1-36

1) Now these are the judgments which thou shalt set before them. (the Israelites)

2) If thou (you) buy an Hebrew servant, six years he (the Hebrew servant) shall serve: and in the seventh he (the Hebrew servant) shall go out free for nothing. (if I remember my United States History correctly, this sounds more like 'Indentured Servitude' or what was called, 'an Indentured Servant'. The man or woman would get on a ship and come to the United States where he or she was sold by the captain of the ship to someone in the United States to be a servant to the one who purchased them. The servant would serve the one who paid their way over to the United States for six years and in the seventh year they would be 'freed' from the contract of being a servant. Their journey to the United States was 'paid in full'. Remember what Heavenly Angel Lay Lay said, 'Look at the characteristics, not the titles'. More about that in my book, MATTHEW'S WORD 'TWO':REAL WORD OF GOD BIBLE)

3) If he (the Hebrew servant) came in by himself, he

(the Hebrew servant) shall go out by himself: if he (the Hebrew servant) were married, then his wife shall go out with him.

4) If his (the Hebrew servant's) master have given him (the Hebrew servant) a wife, and she have born him sons or daughters; the wife and her children shall be her master's, and he (the Hebrew servant) shall go out by himself.

5) And if the servant shall plainly say, I love my master, my wife, and my children; I will not go out free: (the servant chooses to stay in bondage to the master. Sounds like Christians choosing to serve Jesus out of our own free-will)

6) Then his master shall bring him (the servant) unto the judges; he (the master) shall also bring him to the door, or unto the door post; and his master shall bore his (the servant's) ear through with an aul; and he (the servant) shall serve him (the master) for ever. (this sounds like Christianity. We choose to serve Jesus forever and Jesus changes our 'bloodline' with His Supernatural Blood to the 'Spiritual Bloodline with his Supernatural Blood running through our veins.   More about this subject in my book, 'MATTHEW'S WORD 'TWO':REAL WORD OF GOD BIBLE)

7) And if a man sell his daughter to be a maidservant, she (the maidservant) shall not go out as the menservants do.

8) If she (the maidservant) please not her master (doesn't fully satisfy her master), who hath betrothed (married) her (the maidservant) to himself (the master), then shall he (the master) let her (the maidservant) be redeemed (make the maidservant acceptable, or restore her reputation): to sell her (the maidservant) unto a strange nation he (the master) shall have no power, seeing he (the master) hath dealt

deceitfully with her. (taken her virtue, virginity, from the maidservant and then wanted nothing to do with the maidservant)

9) And if he (the master) have betrothed (married) her (the master) unto his (the master's) son, he (the master) shall deal with her (the maidservant) after the manner of daughters.

10) If he (the master) take him (the master) another wife; her (the master's previous wife's) food, her (the master's previous wife's) raiment, and her (the master's previous wife's) duty of marriage, shall he (the master) not diminish.

11) And if he (the master) do not these three unto her, then shall she (the master's previous wife) go out free (no longer bound to the master) without money.

12) He (anyone) that smiteth (hits or beats) a man (or woman), so that he (the man or woman who is being hit) die, shall be surely put to death. (the man or woman who beats the other man to death will be put to death himself. Remember what Heavenly Angel Lay Lay said about the masculine tense of the word meaning both sexes? The masculine tense dominates as the man dominates. More about this in my book, MATTHEW'S WORD 'TWO':REAL WORD OF GOD BIBLE)

13) And if a man lie not in wait (if the man is not scheming to beat up or kill the other man), but God deliver him (the man who is to be killed) into his (the man who is to take the other man's life) hand; then I will appoint thee (God will help the man who killed the other man for going against God's commandments) a place whither he (the man who killed the man who broke God's commandment) shall flee. (God will hide the man who took the other man's life for the sake of keeping God's commandment)

14) But if a man come presumptuously (rude, arrogant, disrespectful, taking action when not authorized to do so) upon his neighbour, to slay him with guile (cunning or being deceitful, just like the serpent did in the Garden of Eden with Eve. Remember why Heavenly Angel Lay Lay said it was only Eve who the serpent tricked? That's in my book, MATTHEW'S WORD 'TWO':REAL WORD OF GOD BIBLE); thou shalt take him (the cunning and deceitful man) from mine altar, that he (the cunning and deceitful man) may die.

15) And he that smiteth (hits them hard) his father, or his mother, shall be surely put to death. (now we need to remember something here. God is talking to Moses and having Moses tell the Israelites these things. The Israelites are following God at this time. The fathers and mothers are obeying God's commandments. This verse does not refer to a father or mother who is making their child to un-Christian things and think the father or mother can get away with it merely because they are the child's father or mother. If a father or mother or anyone else for that matter is making the child do something that is not Godly such as incest, adultery, pornography, strip teasing, fondling of the body of anyone, then the child has a biblical right not only to hit the father or mother or whoever is wanting or making the child do those things and run for help, but also to turn their father or mother or whoever it is into the authorities for prosecution of the law. So many non-Christian parents or members of the family use this particular scripture or a scripture like it to get their children, step-children, adopted children to do non-Christian things and tell the children the children are supposed to allow it because it the Word of God. If your father or mother or anyone else is doing that to you, it's not

God's will for you to put up with it. Call the authorities, get help, just because they are your father, mother, step-father, step-mother, adopted father, adopted mother, step-brothers, step-sisters, adopted brothers, adopted sisters, or anyone else any right whatsoever to touch a child in a sexual manner, fondle your private parts, make you touch them or fondle their private parts or anything else along these lines, not even have the child show off their body in any sexual manner to anyone. Kissing on the cheeks or lips in the spirit of love a parent and child relationship is good, but that's where the line is drawn, not even putting their tongue in your mouth or your tongue in their mouth is right, that's a sexual thing that needs to be stopped. I was twenty-two years old when my dad died, back in 1982, and to the day he died I would give him a peck on his lips and say, 'Dad, I love you.' Dad would always give me a peck back and say, 'I love you too son.' because of our father/son relationship. My dad and I were very close, but not anything in any type of a sexual manner. To this day, I'm forty-eight years old and my mother is seventy-six. Every time I see her I give her a big hug and a peck on her lips when we first see each other and when she leaves or I leave I always tell her, 'I don't know if I will see you again, but if I don't, I want you to know I love you and I appreciate everything you have done for me and helped me all those times I needed help.' and then I give her a big hug and a peck on her lips and she always says back to me, 'I know you do.' and then she give me a big hug and a peck on the lips back. To my boys I have never said 'good bye' to them. I have always given them a peck on their lips and said, 'I love you and I'll see you later honey.' I did this for a reason. I didn't know when I would see them again, or how much later, just that I would see them later and then I gave them a hug and a peck on their lips)

16) And he that stealeth a man (this sounds like Slave Traders. The Slave Traders would unlawfully take a man, woman, or child from their country and sell them in the United States), and selleth him (the man, woman, or child who was stolen), or if he (the man, woman, or child who was stolen) be found in his (the one who stole the man, woman, or child) hand, he (the thief) shall surely be put to death.

17) And he (man, woman, or child) that curseth his father, or his mother, shall surely be put to death. (now remember what I said in Verse 15 above, only Christians. God is talking to the Israelites and they want to serve God and obey His commandments. This does not allow a father, mother, step-father, step-mother, adopted father, adopted mother , step brothers or step sister, adopted brothers, or adopted sisters, or anyone else a right to touch a child in a sexual manner or even have that child show off the child's body in any type of sexual manner to anyone or do anything to a child that is against the Word of God. God is not going to hold it against the child if they are making a child do non-Biblical things)

18) And if men strive (fight against each other) together, and one smite (beats) another with a stone, or with his fist, and he (the one that is beaten) die not, but keepeth his bed (bedridden, forced to stay in bed for any period of time that is not normal, unable to work):

19) If he (that man that was beaten and bedridden, unable to work) rise again, and walk abroad (around) upon his staff (a cane, crutch, etc), then shall he that smote him be quit (the one who beat the one that was bedridden will be finished with his responsibility to the one that was bedridden): only he (that one who

did the hitting) shall pay for the loss of his (the one who was bedridden) time, and shall cause him (the one who was bedridden) to be thoroughly healed. (this sounds like insurance companies, doesn't it)

20) And if a man smite (beats) his servant, or his maid, with a rod, and he (the servant or maid) die under his (the master's) hand; he (the master) shall be surely punished.

21) Notwithstanding (in spite of the fact), if he (the servant or the maid) continue a day or two, he (the master) shall not be punished: for he (the servant) is his (the master's) money.

22) If men strive (fight), and hurt a woman with child, so that her fruit (unborn child) depart from her (the unborn child leaves her womb), and yet no mischief follow (the woman lives): he (the one that caused her to have the miscarriage) shall be surely punished (pressing charges against the one who caused the miscarriage), according as the woman's husband will lay upon him (notice the woman's husband says what the punishment will be to the one who causes the miscarriage, the woman's husband is 'one flesh' with his wife and is biblically responsible to protect his wife. Also remember what Heavenly Angel Lay Lay said about a biblical marriage in my book, MATTHEW'S WORD 'TWO':REAL WORD OF GOD BIBLE, it doesn't take a Marriage Certificate to be a husband and wife. The unborn child is not just her child, but his as well); and he (the one who caused the miscarriage) shall pay as the judges determine. (all those doctors in the practice of aborting babies need to pay according to what the baby's father says, not the law, not the mother, but the baby's father. If the judges don't abide by the father's wishes, then the judges are to be held accountable for the baby's death)

23) And if any mischief follow (if the mother dies also), then thou shalt give life for life,

24) Eye for eye, tooth for tooth, hand for hand, foot for foot,

25) Burning for burning, wound for wound, stripe for stripe.

26) And if a man (master) smite (hurts) the eye of his servant, or the eye of his maid, that it (the eye) perish; he (the master) shall let him (the servant or maid) go free for his eye's sake.

27) And if he (the master) smite (knocks) out his manservant's tooth, or his maidservant's tooth; he (the master) shall let him (the servant or maidservant) go free for his tooth's sake.

28) If an ox (an animal) gore (puncture with their horn) a man or a woman, that they (the man or woman) die: then the ox (the animal) shall be surely stoned (killed), and his flesh (the flesh of the animal) shall not be eaten; but the owner of the ox (the animal) shall be quit. (the owner's debt will be settled)

29) But if the ox (the animal) were wont to push with his horn in time past (if the ox has punctured someone before), and it hath been testified to his owner, and he (the owner) hath not kept him (the animal) in, but that he (the animal) hath killed a man or a woman; the ox (the animal) shall be stoned, and his (the oxen's) owner also shall be put to death.

30) If there be laid on (offered to) him (the owner) a sum of money, then he (the owner) shall give for the ransom of his life (to spare the owner's life) whatsoever is laid upon him. (the owner)

31) Whether he (the animal) have gored (killed) a son, or have gored (killed) a daughter, according to this judgment shall it be done unto him (the animal).

32) If the ox (animal) shall push a manservant or a

maidservant; he (the owner of the animal) shall give unto their (the manservant or maidservant's) master thirty shekels of silver, and the ox (animal) shall be stoned.

33) And if a man shall open a pit, or if a man shall dig a pit, and not cover it, and an ox or an ass (animal) fall therein;

34) The owner of the pit shall make it good, and give money unto the owner of them; and the dead beast shall be his (the owner of the pit).

35) And if one man's ox (animal) hurt another's, that he (the animal) die; then they (the owners) shall sell the live ox (animal), and divide the money of it (the sale of the live oxen); and the dead ox (animal) also they shall divide.

36) Or if it be known (there has been problems keeping the animal fenced in) that the ox (the animal) hath used to push in time past (escaped through the fence), and his owner hath not kept him in (not been able to keep the animal fenced in); he shall surely pay ox for ox (animal for animal); and the dead shall be his own.

Exodus 22:1-31

1) If a man shall steal an ox, or a sheep, and kill it, or sell it; he shall restore five oxen for an ox, and four sheep for a sheep. (an ox is worth more than a sheep, the ox is a work animal)

2) If a thief be found breaking up (broken bones), and be smitten (beaten up) that he die, there shall no blood be shed for him (the thief).

3) If the sun be risen upon him (if the thief was caught after sunrise), there shall be blood shed for him (retrieve the thief to the extent of fighting to get the thief back for trial); for he should make full restitution (pay for what the thief stole); if he (the

thief) have nothing, then he (the thief) shall be sold for his theft.

4) If the theft be certainly found in his (the thief's) hand alive, whether it be ox, or ass, or sheep; he (the thief) shall restore double. (if the thief is caught with the evidence, or the animal still on the leash and leading the animal somewhere, the thief will restore double)

5) If a man shall cause a field or vineyard to be eaten, and shall put in his beast, and shall feed in another man's field; of the best of his own field, and of the best of his own vineyard, shall he make restitution. (the man will pay for portion of the field or vineyard that his beast or animal has eaten)

6) If fire break out, and catch in thorns, so that the stacks of corn, or the standing corn, or the field, be consumed therewith; he that kindled the fire shall surely make restitution.   (if someone causes something to catch on fire and causes damage, whether intentional or accidental, the one who causes the fire will pay for the damage caused by the fire)

7) If a man shall deliver unto his neighbour money or stuff to keep (anything of value), and it (whatever it is that is of value) be stolen out of the man's house; if the thief be found, let him (the thief) pay double.

8) If the thief be not found, then the master of the house shall be brought unto (in front of) the judges, to see whether he (the master of the house) have put his hand (the master's hand) unto his neighbour's goods.

9) For all manner of trespass (breaking a moral or social law), whether it be for ox, for ass, for sheep, for raiment, or for any manner of lost thing which another challengeth to be his (a question of who a certain thing or possession belongs to), the cause (the dispute) of both parties shall come before the judges;

and whom the judges shall condemn (find guilty), he (the guilty one) shall pay double unto his neighbour.

10) If a man deliver unto his neighbour an ass, or an ox, or a sheep, or any beast, to keep; and it die (the animal die) , or be hurt, or driven away, no man seeing it (with no witnesses):

11) Then shall an oath of the LORD be between them both (in today's time, the men were 'sworn in under oath', an oath back then was actually worth something, an oath now days isn't worth the paper it's written on or the time it takes to make a promise), that he (the keeper of the animal) hath not put his hand (harmed) unto his neighbour's goods (the owner's animal); and the owner of it (the animal) shall accept thereof, and he (the keeper for the owner of the animal) shall not make it (the loss of the animal) good.

12) And if it (the animal) be stolen from him (the keeper of the animal), he (the keeper) shall make restitution unto the owner thereof.

13) If it (the animal) be torn in pieces, then let him (the keeper of the animal) bring it (the carcass of the animal, or the remains) for witness (evidence), and he (the keeper of the animal) shall not make good that which was torn.

14) And if a man borrow ought (an animal) of his neighbour, and it (the animal) be hurt (the animal gets hurt while in the possessing of another man), or die, the owner thereof being not with it (if the owner of the animal isn't there with the animal at the time the animal is hurt), he (the one who borrowed the animal) shall surely make it (pay for the animal's wounds or replace the animal if the animal dies) good.

15) But if the owner thereof be with it (if the owner of the animal is there at the time something happens

to the animal), he (the one who borrows the animal) shall not make it good (not pay for the injuries of the animal or replace the animal): if it be an hired thing (if the animal was hired to do a job), it came for his hire (all the debt is already paid for through the money the owner of the animal accepted for the hiring of the animal).

16) And if a man entice (make an offer) a maid that is not betrothed (married), and lie with her (make love to the woman), he (the man) shall surely endow (accept) her to be his wife.

17) If her (the woman's) father utterly refuse to give her (the woman) unto him (the man who has already made love to her), he (the man) shall pay money (to the woman's father) according to the dowry of virgins (the amount of money for a virgin).

18) Thou shalt not suffer (allow) a witch to live. (I want everyone to notice something here. All the other passages usually have several scriptures with each passage. A scripture or two for this reason, a scripture or two for that reason. This particular passage and a very few like it have only one scripture, there is no if's, and's, or but's about it. God said flat out, **THOU SHALT NOT SUFFER, OR ALLOW, A WITCH TO LIVE, PERIOD!!!** Wouldn't you say, God is trying to tell us something here? **UNDER NO CIRCUMSTANCES ARE WE TO ALLOW ANY WITCH TO LIVE!!!** To be that bold and that blunt about something, God must have a reason for that flat-out statement)

19) Whosoever lieth (has sex) with a beast shall surely be put to death. (here is another scripture with no if's, and's, or but's about it. **ANYONE WHO HAS SEX WITH A BEAST, ANY BEAST, IS TO BE PUT TO DEATH!!!** A human having sex with a

beast is an abomination and a part of Satanism even the act is not called Satanism. This is explained in detail in my book MATTHEW'S WORD 'TWO':HEAVENLY ANGEL LAY LAY:REAL WORD OF GOD BIBLE)

20) He (anyone) that sacrificeth unto any god, save unto the LORD only, he (the person who sacrifices to another god) shall be utterly destroyed. (you notice in this scripture, God says, 'destroyed', ruined, abolished, crushed, no more power)

21) Thou shalt neither vex (agitate) a stranger, nor oppress (inflict stress on) him: for ye (you) were strangers in the land of Egypt.

22) Ye (you) shall not afflict (cause distress to) any widow, or fatherless child. (now here we need to do some explaining. Why? Because there are a lot of women in the United States who believe they are widows with fatherless children just because they are divorced. That's not true. **JUST BECAUSE YOU ARE DIVORCED DOES NOT MAKE YOU A WIDOW OR YOUR CHILDREN FATHERLESS.** I have talked to a some real widows and all have said the same thing. The real widows and widowers really get angry when someone says they are a widow or widower and their reasoning is because their ex-spouse, or ex-boyfriend or ex-girlfriend is no longer with them, usually due to a divorce for one reason or another, of course in the court room its always 'irreconcilable differences'. If your ex or your child's mother or father is still alive even though they are not living with you or even living in your area you are not a widow or widower according to Biblical Standards and your child is not fatherless or motherless according to Biblical Standards. Just because there is no one in your life to take their place doesn't make you a widow or widower or your child

fatherless or motherless)

23) If thou (you) afflict (harm) them (the widow or widower, fatherless or motherless child) in any wise, and they (the widow or widower, fatherless or motherless child) cry at all (even the slightest whimper) unto me (God), I will surely hear their cry (the cry of the widow or widower or the fatherless or motherless child);   (Wow, there are a lot of companies who need to see this one, the companies who take the money and inflict the widows and widowers and the fatherless and the motherless children making excuses there is no insurance, there in no food, their lights get turned off, their electricity gets turned off, their taxes go up, all because of the big companies and the government does nothing to stop them. You see, the scripture says, if anyone, it doesn't just say the individuals, it includes the big companies ran by the boards of directors, the electors, this scripture says **ANYONE**)

24) And my (God's) **wrath** (see, here is another scripture that says God definitely gets angry) **shall wax hot** (God won't hold His anger back), and I will kill you (God is KILLING the ones who take and steal afflict the widow, widower, and the fatherless and motherless) with the sword (use of force); and your wives shall be widows, and your children fatherless.   (those who afflict or harm the real widows and widowers and fatherless or motherless shall die and their spouses and children will know what it feels like to feel like the ones you afflicted and harmed. This reminds me of a man who recently passed away after swindling millions from people from a major company, I believe he was actually found guilty of the crime but died before the sentencing could be carried out)

25) If thou (you) lend money to any of my people

(notice God says, **HIS PEOPLE**, His children, His fiance) that is poor by thee (because you have taken their money from them to begin with), thou shalt not be to him as an usurer (you better not treat them like their being poor and broke isn't your fault), neither shalt thou lay upon him usury (you better not charge them any interest).

26) If thou (you) at all take thy (your) neighbour's raiment (clothes) to pledge (as collateral), thou shalt deliver it unto (give it back to) him by that the sun goeth down (by sunset):

27) For that is his covering only, it is his raiment for his skin: wherein shall he sleep (now this verse indicates that the Israelites used their clothes to sleep in and that proves what I said in a previous book about Noah being asleep and Ham coming in and having sex with Noah's wife, Ham's mother. Ham saw Noah's nakedness, remember? Noah was covered by his clothes so Noah being totally naked wasn't what that scripture was talking about, this scripture confirms that Noah had his clothes on when Ham came in and had sex with Noah's wife, Ham's mother, that's why Noah cursed Ham's firstborn, Canaan)? and it shall come to pass, when he (the one whose clothes were taken) crieth unto me, that I will hear; for I am gracious.

28) Thou (you) shalt not revile (swear at) the gods, nor curse the ruler of thy (your) people. (Again, remember, God is talking to the Israelites, those who want to follow Him and serve Him)

29) Thou (you) shalt not delay to offer the first of thy (your) ripe fruits, and of thy (your) liquors: the firstborn of thy (your) sons shalt thou (you) give unto me. (all those Christians who save up their tithes and offerings until they feel they have enough to give to charity, whether it be a church or other charity, that's

not what you need to do. See, this scripture says, 'you are not to delay to offer the first tenth of your blessings)

30) Likewise shalt thou (you) do with thine (your) oxen, and with thy (your) sheep: seven days it (the baby) shall be with his dam (mother); on the eighth day thou shalt give it (the baby animal) me.

31) And ye (you) shall be holy men unto me: neither shall ye (you) eat any flesh that is torn of beasts in the field; ye (you) shall cast it (the torn flesh of the mutilated animal) to the dogs.

Exodus 23:1-33

1) Thou (you) shalt not raise a false report (give a lie for a testimony, police report, or investigation): put not thine hand (do not side) with the wicked to be an unrighteous witness.

2) Thou (you) shalt not follow a multitude (the crowd) to do evil; neither shalt thou (you) speak in a cause (a reason) to decline (to lower oneself to a lower standard) after (following) many to wrest (alter something's meaning) judgment (to get the results you want): (there is an old saying, 'the ends never justifies the means'. In other words, its not right to do whatever it takes to get the end results if the way you get the end results is not good and just. The ends never justifies the means)

3) Neither shalt thou countenance (tolerate) a poor man in his cause (the reason the poor is poor). (in other words, we are not to put up with businesses or laws making the poor, poorer and helping the rich get richer)

4) If thou (you) meet thine (your) enemy's ox or his ass going astray (wandering around), thou (you) shalt surely bring it back to him again.

5) If thou (you) see the ass (animal) of him that

hateth (someone who hates) thee (you) lying under his burden (laying down with packs on), and wouldest forbear (be tolerant) to help him (the one who hates you), thou shalt surely help with him (the work animal who is lying down with the work packs on his back).

6) Thou shalt not wrest (get) the judgment of thy (your) poor in his cause (legal case). (in other words, when the poor wins his case, give him all that was rewarded to him by the judge)

7) Keep thee (yourself) far from a false matter; and the innocent and righteous slay thou not (will not harm you): for I (God) will not justify the wicked.

8) And thou (you) shalt **take no gift** (today's politicians should read this scripture and a lot of that 'soft money' would stop): for **the gift blindeth (blinds) the wise, and perverted (twists) the words of the righteous.**

9) Also thou shalt not oppress a stranger: for ye (you) know the heart of a stranger, seeing ye (you) were strangers in the land of Egypt.

10) And six years thou (you) shalt sow (plant) thy (your) land, and shalt gather in the fruits thereof:

11) But the seventh year thou (you) shalt let it (the ground) rest and lie still; that the poor of thy (your) people may eat: and what they leave the beasts of the field shall eat. In like manner thou (you) shalt deal with thy (your) vineyard, and with thy (your) oliveyard.

12) Six days thou (you) shalt do thy (your) work, and on the seventh day thou (you) shalt rest: that thine (your) ox and thine (your) ass may rest, and the son of thy (your) handmaid, and the stranger, may be refreshed.

13) And in all things that I have said unto you be circumspect [(prudent: showing unwillingness to act

without first weighing the risks or consequences) (Encarta ® World English Dictionary © & (P) 1998-2004 Microsoft Corporation. All rights reserved.)]: and make no mention of the name of other gods, neither let it (any mention of any other god) be heard out of thy (your) mouth.

14) Three times thou (you) shalt keep a feast unto me in the year.

15) Thou (you) shalt keep the feast of unleavened bread: (thou shalt eat unleavened bread seven days, as I commanded thee, in the time appointed of the month Abib; for in it thou camest out from Egypt: and none shall appear before me empty:)

16) And the feast of harvest, the firstfruits of thy (your) labours, which thou (you) hast sown (planted) in the field: and the feast of ingathering (harvesting), which is in the end of the year, when thou (you) hast gathered in thy (your) labours out of the field.

17) Three times in the year all thy (your) males shall appear before the LORD God.

18) Thou (you) shalt not offer the blood of my sacrifice with leavened bread; neither shall the fat of my sacrifice remain until the morning.

19) The first of the firstfruits of thy (your) land thou (you) shalt bring into the house of the LORD thy God. Thou (you) shalt not seethe (make angry) a kid in his mother's milk. (in other words, allow the kid to finish eating his mother's milk)

20) Behold, I send an Angel before thee (you), to keep thee (you) in the way, and to bring thee (you) into the place which I have prepared.

21) Beware of him (the angel), and obey his (the angel's) voice, provoke him (the angel) not; for he (the angel) will not pardon (forgive) your transgressions (wrong deeds): for my name (God) is in him (the angel). (in other words the angel, like

God, has the power and will use that power to keep God's commandments, even to the point of killing the person)

22) But if thou (you) shalt indeed obey his (the angel's) voice, and do all that I speak; then I will be an enemy unto thine (your) enemies, and an adversary unto thine (your) adversaries. (in other words, you do as God says and He will help you in battles to victory, but if you don't do as God says, He won't help you at all)

23) For mine Angel shall go before thee (you), and bring thee (you) in unto the Amorites, and the Hittites, and the Perizzites, and the Canaanites, the Hivites, and the Jebusites: and I will cut them off.

24) Thou (you) shalt not bow down to their gods, nor serve them, nor do after their works: but thou (you) shalt utterly overthrow them, and quite break down their images.

25) And ye (you) shall serve the LORD your God, and he (God) shall bless thy (your) bread, and thy (your) water; and I will take sickness away from the midst of thee.

26) There shall nothing cast their young, nor be barren, in thy (your) land: the number of thy (your) days I will fulfil.

27) I will send my fear before thee (you), and will destroy all the people to whom thou (you) shalt come, and I will make all thine (your) enemies turn their backs unto thee (you).

28) And I will send hornets before thee (you), which shall drive out the Hivite, the Canaanite, and the Hittite, from before thee (you).

29) I will not drive them out from before thee (you) in one year; lest (or else) the land become desolate, and the beast of the field multiply against thee (you). (now here is an interesting verse, God does promise

and He fulfills that promise, but not all at once, over a period of time for a good reason. Now days, just like Heavenly Angel Lay Lay said, we want the promise to come to us right now, but we aren't ready for that blessing yet, He has to prepare us for the blessing before He can give the blessing to us or else the blessing will do us no good because we won't be able to handle the blessing. Read more about this in my book, MATTHEW'S WORD 'TWO':REAL WORD OF GOD BIBLE)

30) By little and little I will drive them (your enemies) out from before thee (you), until thou (you) be increased, and inherit the land.

31) And I will set thy (your) bounds from the Red sea even unto the sea of the Philistines, and from the desert unto the river: for I will deliver the inhabitants of the land into your hand; and thou (you) shalt drive them out before thee (you).

32) Thou (you) shalt make no covenant (contract or agreement) with them, nor with their gods.

33) They shall not dwell in thy (your) land, lest they make thee (you) sin against me: for if thou (you) serve their gods, it will surely be a snare unto thee (you).

Exodus 24:1-18

1) And he (God) said unto Moses, Come up unto the LORD, thou (you), and Aaron, Nadab, and Abihu, and seventy of the elders of Israel; and worship ye (you) afar off.

2) And Moses alone shall come near the LORD: but they (the other people) shall not come nigh (close); neither shall the people go up with him (Moses).

3) And Moses came and told the people all the words of the LORD, and all the judgments: and all the people answered with one voice, and said, All the

words which the LORD hath said will we do.

4) And Moses wrote all the words of the LORD, and rose up early in the morning, and builded an altar under the hill, and twelve pillars, according to the twelve tribes of Israel.

5) And he (Moses) sent young men of the children of Israel, which offered burnt offerings, and sacrificed peace offerings of oxen unto the LORD.

6) And Moses took half of the blood, and put it in basons; and half of the blood he (Moses) sprinkled on the altar.

7) And he (Moses) took the book of the covenant, and read in the audience of the people: and they (all the people) said, All that the LORD hath said will we do, and be obedient.

8) And Moses took the blood, and sprinkled it (the blood) on the people, and said, Behold the blood of the covenant, which the LORD hath made with you concerning all these words.

9) Then went up Moses, and Aaron, Nadab, and Abihu, and seventy of the elders of Israel:

10) And they (Moses, Aaron, Nadab, and Abihu) saw the God of Israel (now did they really see God? Yes and no, what do I mean? Look a the scripture, yes, they did see God, but not all of God. It continues): and there was under his (God's) feet as it were a paved work of a sapphire stone (ok, now we know they saw God's feet), and as it were the body of heaven in his clearness (ok, now we know they saw some sort of His body as we, humans, would be able to accept it in our carnal minds).

11) And upon the nobles of the children of Israel he (God) laid not his hand: also they (now the nobles are in on the action) saw God, and did eat and drink. (everyone is seeing one part of God and another part of God, but no one actually sees God's face. There

are several people right in this scripture alone that are seeing God. Next time someone tells you no one has ever seen God, tell them they don't know what the are talking about. Their argument is that no one has seen God face to face, that's because God is too powerful for mankind to see face to face and live to tell about it)

12) And the LORD said unto Moses, Come up to me into the mount, and be there (now God is telling Moses to come closer to God, separate from the rest and go up closer): and I will give thee (Moses) tables of stone, and a law, and commandments which I have written (God is writing the tables of stone); that thou (you) mayest teach them (the children of Israel).

13) And Moses rose up, and his minister Joshua: and Moses went up into the mount of God.

14) And he (Moses) said unto the elders, Tarry ye (you stay) here for us, until we come again unto you: and, behold, Aaron and Hur are with you: if any man have any matters (problems) to do (that needs solving), let him (the men) come unto them (go to Aaron and Hur).

15) And Moses went up into the mount, and a cloud covered the mount.

16) And the glory of the LORD abode (stayed) upon mount Sinai, and the cloud covered it (the mount) six days (the cloud is protecting Moses, God's full glory is unable to be seen by mortal man): and the seventh day he (God) called unto Moses out of the midst of the cloud.

17) And the sight of the glory of the LORD was like devouring fire on the top of the mount in the eyes of the children of Israel.

18) And Moses went into the midst of the cloud, and gat (a narrow passage led Moses) him up into the mount: and Moses was in the mount (Moses was

actually in the mount not on the mount) forty days and forty nights.

Exodus 25:1-40
1) And the LORD spake unto Moses, saying,
2) Speak unto the children of Israel, that they bring me an offering: **of every man that GIVETH IT WILLINGLY WITH HIS HEART** ye shall take my offering.
3) And this is the offering which ye (you) shall take of them (the children of Israel); gold, and silver, and brass, (I kept asking myself, does God want gold, silver, and brass? Because that's what the most important thing to the children of Israel was at that particular time. The children of Israel were used to gold, silver, and brass and making 'false gods' with it, those were the most valuable things to the children of Israel at that time. God wanted that stuff out of their system so they could put Him first and worship Him whole heartedly. Not only that, but God had a use for all that with what God was planning)
4) And blue, and purple, and scarlet, and fine linen, and goats' hair, (other treasured items in Egypt)
5) And rams' skins dyed red, and badgers' skins, and shittim wood,
6) Oil for the light, spices for anointing oil, and for sweet incense,
7) Onyx stones, and stones to be set in the ephod [(Hebrew priests' apron: an embroidered garment, believed to be like an apron with shoulder straps, worn by Hebrew priests in ancient Israel) (Encarta ® World English Dictionary © & (P) 1998-2004 Microsoft Corporation. All rights reserved.)], and in the breastplate. [(Jewish priestly garment: a garment worn over the breast by Jewish high priests in ancient times, set with twelve precious stones representing

the twelve tribes of Israel) (Encarta ® World English Dictionary © & (P) 1998-2004 Microsoft Corporation. All rights reserved.)]

8) And let them (the children of Israel) make me (God) a sanctuary [(most sacred part of holy building: the most sacred part of a consecrated building, for example, the area around the altar in a Christian church) (Encarta ® World English Dictionary © & (P) 1998-2004 Microsoft Corporation. All rights reserved.)]; that I may dwell among them (the children of Israel).

9) According to all that I shew thee (show you), after the pattern of the tabernacle, and the pattern of all the instruments thereof, even so shall ye (you) make it (the tabernacle).

10) And they (the children of Israel) shall make an ark of shittim wood [(North American tree with hard wood: a North American tree that has hard dense wood and black fruit.) (Encarta ® World English Dictionary © & (P) 1998-2004 Microsoft Corporation. All rights reserved.)]: two cubits (according to one of my instructors, one cubit is from the tip of a person's forefinger to the back of that same person's elbow. That's the reason whoever starts out measuring must be the only one doing the measuring. In other words, Noah's sons couldn't help Noah measure any of the wood for the Ark, Noah had to do all the measuring himself because his arm wasn't the same length of anyone elses. That's also why when it came to merchants, the merchant always did the measuring because the merchant was selling his goods by the cubit, measuring the linen or whatever it was by the tip of his forefinger to the back of his elbow. The average cubit is approximately 18 inches or one inch being 2.54 cm, 18 inches = 45.72 cm) and a half shall be the length

thereof, and a cubit and a half the breadth thereof, and a cubit and a half the height thereof. (what amazes me is that shittim wood is even over in that part of the world. See, the dictionary says Shittim Wood is in North America, not in Israel, Egypt, or any part of the Earth over there, so where are the Israelites going to get Shittim Wood to begin with?)

11) And thou (you) shalt overlay it (the ark) with pure gold, within and without (inside and out) shalt thou overlay it (the ark), and shalt make upon it (the ark) a crown of gold round about.

12) And thou (you) shalt cast four rings of gold for it (the ark), and put them (the four rings of gold) in the four corners thereof; and two rings shall be in the one side of it (the ark), and two rings in the other side of it (the ark).

13) And thou (you) shalt make staves [(a long thin piece of wood) (Encarta ® World English Dictionary © & (P) 1998-2004 Microsoft Corporation. All rights reserved.)] of shittim wood, and overlay them (the staves) with gold.

14) And thou (you) shalt put the staves into the rings by the sides of the ark, that the ark may be borne (lifted and carried) with them (the staves).

15) The staves shall be in the rings of the ark: they (the staves) shall not be taken from it (the rings of the ark).

16) And thou (you) shalt put into the ark the testimony which I shall give thee (you).

17) And thou (you) shalt make a mercy seat of pure gold: two cubits and a half (36½ inches one inch is 2.54 cm, 36½ inches = 92.71 cm) shall be the length thereof, and a cubit and a half (18½ inches or 46.99 cm) the breadth thereof.

18) And thou (you) shalt make two cherubims [(angel of second order: an angel, specifically one belonging

to the second order of angels in the celestial hierarchy whose distinctive attribute is knowledge) (Encarta ® World English Dictionary © & (P) 1998-2004 Microsoft Corporation. All rights reserved.)] of gold, of beaten work shalt thou (you) make them the cherubims), in the two ends of the mercy seat [(covering for the Ark of the Covenant: the gold covering on the Ark of the Covenant, regarded as God's resting place) (Encarta ® World English Dictionary © & (P) 1998-2004 Microsoft Corporation. All rights reserved.)].

19) And make one cherub (an of the angels of the second order) on the one end, and the other cherub on the other end: even of the mercy seat (the covering for the Ark of the Covenant) shall ye (you) make the cherubims on the two ends thereof.

20) And the cherubims (the angels of the second order) shall stretch forth their wings on high, covering the mercy seat (the covering for the Ark of the Covenant) with their wings, and their faces shall look one to another; toward the mercy seat (the covering for the Ark of the Covenant) shall the faces of the cherubims (the angels of the second order) be.

21) And thou (you) shalt put the mercy seat above upon the ark; and in the ark thou (you) shalt put the testimony that I shall give thee (you).

22) And there I will meet with thee (you), and I will commune with thee (you) from above the mercy seat (the covering of the Ark of the Covenant), from between the two cherubims (angels) which are upon the ark of the testimony, of all things which I will give thee (you) in commandment unto the children of Israel.

23) Thou shalt also make a table of shittim wood: two cubits (36 inches or 91.44 cm) shall be the length thereof, and a cubit (18 inches or 45.72 cm) the

breadth thereof, and a cubit and a half (27 inches or 68.58 cm) the height thereof.

24) And thou (you) shalt overlay it (the table of shittim wood) with pure gold, and make thereto a crown of gold round about (the table of shittim wood).

25) And thou (you) shalt make unto it (the table of shittim wood) a border of an hand breadth round about, and thou (you) shalt make a golden crown to the border thereof round about.

26) And thou (you) shalt make for it (the table of shittim wood) four rings of gold, and put the rings in the four corners that are on the four feet thereof.

27) Over against the border shall the rings be for places of the staves [(a long thin piece of wood) (Encarta ® World English Dictionary © & (P) 1998-2004 Microsoft Corporation. All rights reserved.)] to bear the table.

28) And thou shalt make the staves of shittim wood, and overlay them with gold, that the table may be borne with them.

29) And thou (you) shalt make the dishes thereof, and spoons thereof, and covers thereof, and bowls thereof, to cover withal: of pure gold shalt thou (you) make them (the dishes, spoons, covers, and bowls).

30) And thou (you) shalt set upon the table shewbread [(bread placed in tabernacle: in the Bible, the twelve loaves of bread placed in the tabernacle every Sabbath by the Hebrew priests of ancient Israel) (Encarta ® World English Dictionary © & (P) 1998-2004 Microsoft Corporation. All rights reserved.)] before me **always**. [(every time or continuously: used to indicate that something happens or is done at all times, either continuously, repetitively, or on every occasion) (Encarta ® World

English Dictionary © & (P) 1998-2004 Microsoft Corporation. All rights reserved.) (through all past or future time: throughout all past time or all future time, or for as long as anyone can remember and as long as anyone can foresee) (Encarta ® World English Dictionary © & (P) 1998-2004 Microsoft Corporation. All rights reserved.)]

31) And thou (you) shalt make a candlestick of pure gold: of beaten work [(make by blows: to shape or make something by pounding or trampling) (Encarta ® World English Dictionary © & (P) 1998-2004 Microsoft Corporation. All rights reserved.)] shall the candlestick be made: his (the Ark's) shaft, and his (the Ark's) branches, his (the Ark's) bowls, his (the Ark's) knops (a small decorative knob), and his (the Ark's) flowers, shall be of the same.

32) And six branches shall come out of the sides of it (the Ark of the Covenant); three branches of the candlestick out of the one side, and three branches of the candlestick out of the other side:

33) Three bowls made like unto almonds, with a knop and a flower in one branch; and three bowls made like almonds in the other branch, with a knop and a flower: so in the six branches that come out of the candlestick.

34) And in the candlesticks shall be four bowls made like unto almonds, with their knops and their flowers.

35) And there shall be a knop under two branches of the same, and a knop under two branches of the same, and a knop under two branches of the same, according to the six branches that proceed out of the candlestick.

36) Their knops and their branches shall be of the same: all it shall be one beaten work of pure gold.

37) And thou (you) shalt make the seven lamps thereof: and they shall light the lamps thereof, that

they (the lamps) may give light over against it (the Ark of the Covenant).

38) And the tongs thereof, and the snuffdishes thereof, shall be of pure gold.

39) Of a talent of pure gold shall he make it, with all these vessels.

40) And look that thou (you) make them after their pattern, which was shewed thee in the mount.

Exodus 26:1-37

1) Moreover thou (you) shalt make the tabernacle with ten curtains of fine twined linen, and blue, and purple, and scarlet: with cherubims (angels) of cunning work shalt thou (you) make them (the curtains).

2) The length of one curtain shall be eight and twenty cubits (18 inches x 28 = 504 inches = 42 feet or 504 inches x 2.54 = 1,280.16 cm), and the breadth of one curtain four cubits (4 x 18 = 72 inches = 6 feet or 182.88 cm): and every one of the curtains shall have one measure (system for determining size: a particular system used to determine the dimensions, area, volume, or weight of something) (Encarta ® World English Dictionary © & (P) 1998-2004 Microsoft Corporation. All rights reserved.).

3) The five curtains shall be coupled together one to another; and other five curtains shall be coupled one to another.

4) And thou (you) shalt make loops of blue upon the edge of the one curtain from the selvedge (nonfraying edge of fabric: an edge of a piece of fabric that is woven so that it will not fray) (Encarta ® World English Dictionary © & (P) 1998-2004 Microsoft Corporation. All rights reserved.) in the coupling (1. something that joins two things: something that joins two things, especially a device for connecting two

pieces of pipe, hose, or tube 2. joining two things together: a joining together or linking of two persons or things) (Encarta ® World English Dictionary © & (P) 1998-2004 Microsoft Corporation. All rights reserved.) and likewise shalt thou (you will) make in the uttermost edge of another curtain, in the coupling of the second.

5) Fifty loops shalt thou (you will) make in the one curtain, and fifty loops shalt thou make in the edge of the curtain that is in the coupling of the second; that the loops may take hold one of another.

6) And thou shalt make fifty taches (hooks or clasps) of gold, and couple the curtains together with the taches (hooks or clasps): and it (joined together, the curtains will become) shall be one tabernacle.

7) And thou (you) shalt make curtains of goats' hair to be a covering upon the tabernacle: eleven curtains shalt thou (you) make.

8) The length of one curtain shall be thirty cubits (30 x 18 = 540 inches = 45 feet or 1,371.6 cm), and the breadth of one curtain four cubits 4 x 18 = 72 = 6 feet or 182.88 cm): and the eleven curtains shall be all of one measure (measured by the same system).

9) And thou (you) shalt couple five curtains by themselves, and six curtains by themselves, and shalt double the sixth curtain in the forefront (in the front) of the tabernacle.

10) And thou (you) shalt make fifty loops on the edge of the one curtain that is outmost in the coupling, and fifty loops in the edge of the curtain which coupleth the second.

11) And thou (you) shalt make fifty taches (couplings) of brass, and put the taches (couplings) into the loops, and couple the tent together, that it may be one.

12) And the remnant that remaineth of the curtains of

the tent, the half curtain that remaineth, shall hang over the backside of the tabernacle.

13) And a cubit (18 inches = 1½ feet or 45.72 cm) on the one side, and a cubit on the other side of that which remaineth in the length of the curtains of the tent, it (the remnant or half of the curtain that remains) shall hang over the sides of the tabernacle on this side and on that side, to cover it.

14) And thou (you) shalt make a covering for the tent of rams' skins dyed red, and a covering above of badgers' skins.

15) And thou (you) shalt make boards for the tabernacle of shittim wood standing up.

16) Ten cubits (10 x 18 inches = 180 inches = 15 feet or 457.2 cm) shall be the length of a board, and a cubit and a half (27 inches = 2.25 feet or 68.58 cm) shall be the breadth of one board.

17) Two tenons [(projection on wood for making joint: a projection made on the end of one piece of wood that fits into a mortise on another piece, making a joint) (Encarta ® World English Dictionary © & (P) 1998-2004 Microsoft Corporation. All rights reserved.)] shall there be in one board, set in order one against another: thus shalt thou make (you will make this) for all the boards of the tabernacle.

18) And thou (you) shalt make the boards for the tabernacle, twenty boards on the south side southward.

19) And thou (you) shalt make forty sockets [(shaped hole for connection: a hole or recess in something specially shaped to receive a particular object or part, for example, the hole that receives a light bulb or one that receives a plug on an electrical device) (Encarta ® World English Dictionary © & (P) 1998-2004 Microsoft Corporation. All rights reserved.) of silver under the twenty boards; two sockets under one

board for his two tenons [(projection on wood for making joint: a projection made on the end of one piece of wood that fits into a mortise on another piece, making a joint) (Encarta ® World English Dictionary   ©   &   (P)   1998-2004   Microsoft Corporation. All rights reserved.)], and two sockets under another board for his two tenons.

20) And for the second side of the tabernacle on the north side there shall be twenty boards:

21) And their forty sockets of silver; two sockets under one board, and two sockets under another board.

22) And for the sides of the tabernacle westward thou shalt make six boards.

23) And two boards shalt thou make (you shall make) for the corners of the tabernacle in the two sides.

24) And they (the boards) shall be coupled together beneath, and they (the boards) shall be coupled together above the head of it unto one ring: thus shall it be for them both (the boards); they (the boards) shall be for the two corners.

25) And they (the boards) shall be eight boards, and their sockets of silver, sixteen sockets; two sockets under one board, and two sockets under another board.

26) And thou (you) shalt make bars of shittim wood; five for the boards of the one side of the tabernacle,

27) And five bars for the boards of the other side of the tabernacle, and five bars for the boards of the side of the tabernacle, for the two sides westward.

28) And the middle bar in the midst of the boards shall reach from end to end.

29) And thou (you) shalt overlay the boards with gold, and make their rings of gold for places for the bars: and thou (you) shalt overlay the bars with gold.

30) And thou (you) shalt rear up the tabernacle

according to the fashion thereof which was shewed thee in the mount.

31) And thou (you) shalt make a vail of blue, and purple, and scarlet, and fine twined linen of cunning work: with cherubims (angels) shall it (the vail) be made:

32) And thou (you) shalt hang it (the vail) upon four pillars of shittim wood overlaid with gold: their hooks (the hooks of the vail) shall be of gold, upon the four sockets of silver.

33) And thou (you) shalt hang up the vail under the taches (clasps), that thou (you) mayest bring in thither within the vail the ark of the testimony: and the vail shall divide unto you between the holy place and the most holy.

34) And thou (you) shalt put the mercy seat [(covering for the Ark of the Covenant: the gold covering on the Ark of the Covenant, regarded as God's resting place) (Encarta ® World English Dictionary © & (P) 1998-2004 Microsoft Corporation. All rights reserved.)] upon the ark of the testimony in the most holy place.

35) And thou (you) shalt set the table without the vail, and the candlestick over against the table on the side of the tabernacle toward the south: and thou shalt (you will) put the table on the north side.

36) And thou shalt make an hanging for the door of the tent, of blue, and purple, and scarlet, and fine twined linen, wrought with needlework.

37) And thou shalt make for the hanging five pillars of shittim wood, and overlay them (the five pillars of shittim wood) with gold, and their (the pillars) hooks shall be of gold: and thou shalt cast five sockets of brass for them (the pillars).

Exodus 27:1-21

1) And thou shalt (you will) make an altar of shittim wood, five cubits long (5 x 18 inches = 90 inches = 7.5 feet or 19.05 cm), and five cubits broad (5 x 18 inches = 90 inches = 7.5 feet or 19.05 cm); the altar shall be foursquare: and the height thereof shall be three cubits (3 x 18 = 54 inches = 4½ feet or 54 inches x 2.54 cm per inch = 137.16 cm) (Holman 1991).

2) And thou shalt make the horns [(horn-shaped thing: something shaped like a horn, for example, either of the tips of a crescent moon, the pommel of a saddle, or the pointed end of an anvil) (Encarta ® World English Dictionary © & (P) 1998-2004 Microsoft Corporation. All rights reserved.)] of it (the alter) upon the four corners thereof: his (the alter's) horns shall be of the same: and thou shalt overlay it (the horns) with brass.

3) And thou shalt make his pans to receive his ashes, and his shovels, and his basons, and his fleshhooks, and his firepans: all the vessels thereof thou shalt make of brass.

4) And thou shalt make for it (the horns) a grate of network of brass; and upon the net shalt thou make four brasen rings in the four corners thereof.

5) And thou shalt put it (the horns) under the compass of the altar beneath, that the net may be even to the midst of the altar.

6) And thou shalt make staves for the altar, staves of shittim wood, and overlay them (the staves of shittim wood) with brass.

7) And the staves shall be put into the rings, and the staves shall be upon the two sides of the altar, to bear it (the alter).

8) Hollow with boards shalt thou make it (the alter): as it (the alter) was shewed thee (showed to you) in the mount, so shall they (the craftsmen) make it (the

alter).

9) And thou shalt make the court of the tabernacle: for the south side southward there shall be hangings for the court of fine twined linen of an hundred cubits long for one side:

10) And the twenty pillars thereof and their twenty sockets shall be of brass; the hooks of the pillars and their fillets shall be of silver.

11) And likewise for the north side in length there shall be hangings of an hundred cubits long, and his twenty pillars and their twenty sockets of brass; the hooks of the pillars and their fillets of silver.

12) And for the breadth of the court on the west side shall be hangings of fifty cubits (50 x 18 inches = 900 inches = 75 feet or 2,286 cm): their pillars ten, and their sockets ten.

13) And the breadth of the court on the east side eastward shall be fifty cubits (50 x 18 inches = 900 inches = 75 feet or 2,286 cm).

14) The hangings of one side of the gate shall be fifteen cubits (15 x 18 inches = 270 inches = 22.5 feet or 685.8 cm): their pillars three, and their sockets three.

15) And on the other side shall be hangings fifteen cubits (15 x 18 inches = 270 inches = 22.5 feet or 685.8 cm): their pillars three, and their sockets three.

16) And for the gate of the court shall be an hanging of twenty cubits (20 x 18 inches = 360 inches = 30 feet or 914.4 cm), of blue, and purple, and scarlet, and fine twined linen, wrought with needlework: and their pillars shall be four, and their sockets four.

17) All the pillars round about the court shall be filleted with silver; their hooks shall be of silver, and their sockets of brass.

18) The length of the court shall be an hundred cubits (100 x 18 inches = 1,800 inches = 150 feet or 4,572

cm), and the breadth fifty (50 x 18 inches = 900 inches = 75 feet or 2,286 cm) every where, and the height five cubits (5 x 18 inches = 90 inches = 7.5 feet or 228.6 cm) of fine twined linen, and their sockets of brass.

19) All the vessels of the tabernacle in all the service thereof, and all the pins thereof, and all the pins of the court, shall be of brass.

20) And thou shalt (you will) command the children of Israel, that they bring thee pure oil olive beaten for the light, to cause the lamp to burn always.

21) In the tabernacle of the congregation without the vail, which is before the testimony, Aaron and his sons shall order it from evening to morning before the LORD: it shall be a statute for ever unto their generations on the behalf of the children of Israel.

(CONTINUED IN:
ONE TOO MANY FRIENDS?
IT HAPPENS)

BIBLIOGRAPHY

1. Encarta ® World English Dictionary © & (P) 1998-2004 Microsoft Corporation. All rights reserved.

2. Merriam Webster's Collegiate Dictionary Tenth Edition (1993), United States of America.

3. The Holy Bible King James Version (1998), B. B. Kirkbride Bible Co., Inc. Indianapolis, IN..USA

4. Holman Bible Dictionary (1991), Holman Bible Publishers, Nashville, Tennessee.

www.ingramcontent.com/pod-product-compliance
Lightning Source LLC
LaVergne TN
LVHW091211080426
835509LV00006B/937

9 780615 174884